CENGAGE Learning

Novels for Students, Volume 2

Since this page cannot legibly accommodate all copyright notices, the acknowledgments constitute an extension of the copyright notice.

While every effort has been made to secure permission to reprint material and to ensure the reliability of the information presented in this publication, Gale Research neither guarantees the accuracy of the data contained herein nor assumes any responsibility for errors, omissions or discrepancies. Gale accepts no payment for listing; and inclusion in the publication of any organization, agency, institution, publication, service, or individual does not imply endorsement of the editors or publisher. Errors brought to the attention of the publisher and verified to the satisfaction of the publisher will be corrected in future editions.

This publication is a creative work fully protected by all applicable copyright laws, as well as by misappropriation, trade secret, unfair competition

Copyright © 1997

Gale Research
835 Penobscot Building
645 Griswold St.
Detroit, Ml 48226-4094

This book is printed on acid-free paper that meets the minimum requirements of American National Standard for Information Sciences—Permanence Paper for Printed Library Materials, ANSI Z39.48-1984.

ISBN 0-7876-1687-7
ISSN 1094-3552

Printed in the United States of America
10 9 8 7 6 5 4

Things Fall Apart

Chinua Achebe

1958

Introduction

The story of Chinua Achebe's novel *Things Fall Apart* takes place in the Nigerian village of Umuofia in the late 1880s, before missionaries and other outsiders have arrived. The Ibo clan practices common tribal traditions—worship of gods, sacrifice, communal living, war, and magic. Leadership is based on a man's personal worth and his contribution to the good of the tribe. Okonkwo stands out as a great leader of the Ibo tribe. Tribesmen respect Okonkwo for his many achievements.

Even though the tribe reveres Okonkwo, he must be punished for his accidental shooting of a young tribesman. The Ibo ban Okonkwo from the clan for seven years. Upon his return to the village, Okonkwo finds a tribe divided by the influence of missionaries and English bureaucrats who have interrupted the routine of tradition. Only when Okonkwo commits the ultimate sin against the tribe does the tribe come back together to honor custom.

Critics appreciate Achebe's development of the conflict that arises when tradition clashes with change. He uses his characters and their unique language to portray the double tragedies that occur in the story. Readers identify not only with Okonkwo and his personal hardships but also with the Ibo culture and its disintegration. Chinua Achebe wrote *Things Fall Apart* not for his fellow Nigerians, but for people beyond his native country. He wanted to explain the truth about the effects of losing one's culture. Published in 1958, the book was not widely read by Nigerians or by Africans in general. When Nigeria became independent in 1960, however, Africans appreciated the novel for its important contribution to Nigerian history.

Author Biography

Chinua Achebe is a world-renowned scholar recognized for his ability to write simply, yet eloquently, about life's universal qualities. His writing weaves together history and fiction to produce a literary broadcloth that offers visions of people enduring real life. Critics appreciate his just and realistic treatment of his topics.

Achebe writes primarily about his native Africa, where he was born Albert Chinualumogu Achebe in 1930. He grew up in Ogidi, Nigeria, one of the first centers of Anglican missionary work in Eastern Nigeria. His father and mother, Isaiah and Janet Achebe, were missionary teachers. Achebe's life as a Christian and member of the Ibo tribe enables him to create realistic depictions of both contemporary and pre-colonized Africa. He blends his knowledge of Western political ideologies and Christian doctrine with folklore, proverbs, and idioms from his native tribe to produce stories of African culture that are intimate and authentic.

Achebe left the village of Ogidi to attend Government College in Umuahia, and later, University College in Tbadan. He received his Bachelor of Arts degree from University College in 1953. He worked first for the Nigerian Broadcasting Corpo-ration as a writer and continued radio work in various capacities until 1966, when he resigned from his post as Director of External Broadcasting.

Dissatisfied with the political climate that would later prompt the Biafran War, he began traveling abroad and lectured as the appointed Senior Research Fellow for the University of Nigeria, Nsukka.

Continuing his teaching career, Achebe accepted a position with the University of Massachusetts, Amherst, in 1972. He was a visiting Professor of English at that institution until 1976 and again in 1987–1988. He also spent a year as a visiting professor at the University of Connecticut. In the intervening years, Achebe returned to his native country to teach at the University of Nigeria, Nsukka.

Achebe has written extensively throughout his adult life. His numerous articles, novels, short stories, essays, and children's books have earned prestigious awards. For example, his book of poetry *Christmnas in Biafra* was a winner of the first Commonwealth Poetry Prize. His novels *Arrow of God and Anthills of the Savannah* won, respectively, the New Statesman-Jock Campbell Award and finalist for the 1987 Booker Prize in England.

Achebe continues to write and participate in scholarly activities throughout the world, while making his home in Annandale, New York, with his wife, Christie. They have four children and teach at Bard College.

Part I—Okonkwo's Rise to Fame

Achebe's *Things Fall Apart* describes the tragic demise of an Ibo man named Okonkwo. Initially, Okonkwo rises from humble origins to become a powerful leader in Umuofia, a rural village in south-eastern Nigeria. As Okonkwo climbs the ladder to success, however, it becomes apparent that his strengths are also his weaknesses: his self-confidence becomes pride, his manliness develops into authoritarianism, and his physical strength eventually turns into uncontrolled rage. In a broader sense, Achebe sets this story about Okonkwo at the end of the nineteenth century, when Europeans first began colonizing this region of Nigeria on a large scale. By so doing, Achebe establishes a parallel between Okonkwo's personal tragedy and colonialism's tragic destruction of native African cultures.

The first section of the novel describes Okonkwo's rise to a position of power. Determined to overcome the unmanly and unsuccessful example of his father, Unoka, Okonkwo develops a strength and determination unmatched among his peers. These attributes enable him to become a great wrestler, strong warrior, wealthy farmer, and prestigious member of his community. As the Umuofians notice his extraordinary talents, they reward him with numerous titles and honors. For example, they make him the guardian of Ikemefuna, a young boy awarded to Umuofia as compensation for wrongs committed by a neighboring village. Similarly, when Okonkwo starts a farm, he receives a generous loan of 800 yams from Nwakibie, a wealthy farmer. Nwakibie is willing to loan these yams to Okonkwo because he knows that Okonkwo will succeed. Okonkwo proves his ability to succeed by surviving even after a terrible drought destroys his crops. Undaunted by either his humble origins or the forces of nature, Okonkwo soon becomes one of the most successful and well respected men in Umuofia.

Okonkwo's success, however, quickly begins to lead toward his ultimate downfall. Because he is so successful, he has little patience with unsuccessful and "unmanly" men like his father. In fact, he publicly insults Osugo, a less successful man, by calling him a woman during a kindred meeting. Not only does Okonkwo's success lead to conflicts with other members of the village, but it also drastically disrupts his ability to rule his own family. Because of his autocratic style of ruling and impulsive anger, his own family fears him. In fact, his own son, Nwoye, eventually rejects him, much like Okonkwo had rejected his own father earlier— only Nwoye rejects Okonkwo for being excessively masculine, whereas Okonkwo rejected Unoka for not being manly enough. Even more significantly, Okonkwo's hasty temper provokes him to beat his third wife, Ojiugo, during the sacred Week of Peace, a festival time during which Ibo custom strictly forbids any form of violence. Okonkwo commits his worst crime, however, when he participates in the sacrifice of Ikemefuna. After Okonkwo had raised Ikemefuna as his own son for several years, an Oracle required that the Umuofians sacrifice Ikemefuna. Because Okonkwo had been like a father to Ikemefuna, Okonkwo's friend Ezeudu warns him not to participate in the sacrifice. When the rest of the men begin sacrificing Ikemefuna, however, Okonkwo disregards Ezeudu's advice and participates in the sacrifice because he fears that the others might consider him unmanly. When Nwoye eventually finds out about Ikemefuna's death, he has a serious crisis that causes him to question not only his father's example but also the customs and beliefs of his people.

Despite Okonkwo's numerous violations of custom and violent behavior, he ultimately loses his prestigious position in Umuofia not because of his misdeeds but because of an accident. During Ezeudu's funeral ceremony, his gun misfires and accidentally kills a boy. Ironically, it is for this accident rather than for his numerous misdeeds that the Umuofians burn down Okonkwo's home and exile him for a period of seven years.

Part II—Okonkwo's Exile to Mbanta

After being exiled from Umuofia, Okonkwo seeks refuge among his mother's kinsmen in Mbanta, a neighboring village. During this time, the

British begin colonizing the surrounding areas, and this begins a vicious cycle of mutual confrontation as the two cultures clash. For example, the inhabitants of Abame kill the first white man who arrives in their city because they fear him and cannot communicate with him, and the British destroy Abame in retaliation for this murder. Christian missionaries also begin arriving in Umuofia and Mbanta, and they hold debates to gain converts. Most of the people are not interested in the missionaries' religion, but a few people, including Okonkwo's son Nwoye, convert. When Okonkwo finds out about Nwoye's conversion, he becomes enraged and disowns Nwoye. Toward the end of Okonkwo's exile, the tensions between the village and the missionaries escalate when the Christian converts kill a sacred python and the tribe retaliates by ostracizing the Christians. After Okonkwo's period of exile ends, he holds a great feast to thank his relatives, and he begins making preparations for his return to Umuofia.

Part III—Okonkwo's Return to Umuofia

In the final section, Okonkwo returns from exile with hopes of reclaiming a position of power in Umuofia, but Umuofia has changed drastically since the arrival of the Europeans. The first missionary in Umuofia, Mr. Brown, won the people's admiration because he respected their customs and developed personal relationships with them. When Mr. Brown has to leave for health reasons, however, he is replaced by the Reverend James Smith, an ethnocentric zealot who stirs up deep antagonism between the new Christian converts and the rest of the town. These tensions finally explode when Enoch, an overzealous new convert, eats a sacred python and publicly unmasks an egwugwu spirit. The Umuofians avenge Enoch's blasphemies by burning down the Christian church, and the British retaliate in turn by arresting the leaders of Umuofia and fining them 200 bags of cowries.

The Umuofians pay the fine, but the leaders are angered by the duplicitous and unjust manner in which the District Commissioner treated them. Consequently, they hold a meeting to decide how to respond. The village is divided as to whether they should ignore this injustice or retaliate with violence, but Okonkwo has made up his mind that he will oppose British colonization even if nobody else will join him. When a messenger from the government arrives to stop their meeting, Okonkwo kills the messenger, and the meeting ends in chaos.

The next day the District Commissioner himself comes to arrest Okonkwo, but Okonkwo has already committed suicide. The people of Umuofia ask the commissioner to bury Okonkwo because it is against their custom to bury a man who has committed suicide. The commissioner orders his men to take down Okonkwo's body because he has an interest in African customs, but he refuses to help personally because he fears that cutting down a dead body might give the natives a poor opinion of him. Achebe's bitterly ironic conclusion to the novel describes the District Commissioner's callous response to Okonkwo's tragedy.

> In the many years that he had toiled to bring civilization to different parts of Africa he had learnt a number of things. One of them was that a District Commissioner must never attend to such undignified details as cutting down a hanged man from the trees. Such attention would give the natives a poor opinion of him. In the book which he planned to write he would stress that point. As he walked back to the court he thought about that book. Every day brought him some new material. The story of this man who had killed a messenger and hanged himself would make interesting reading. One could almost write a whole chapter on him. Perhaps not a whole chapter but a reasonable paragraph, at any rate. There was so much else to include, and one must be firm in cutting out the details. He had already chosen the title of the book, after much thought: *The Pacification of the Primitive Tribes of the Lower Niger.*

Ironically, the District Commissioner thinks that he has helped pacify the "primitive" tribes of the Lower Niger, but he is blind to his complicity in destroying these tribes and provoking the chain of events leading to Okonkwo's suicide. The District Commissioner's thoughts are doubly ironic because he claims to understand Africa enough to write a history of it, but he remains thoroughly ignorant of the people he intends to write about. Okonkwo's tragic demise, like the tragic destruction of indigenous African people and their traditions, is a long and complex history. Unfortunately, the District Commissioner only sees it as a mere paragraph. For far too long, Europeans like the District Commissioner have ignored and misrepresented the history of Africa, but Achebe's *Things Fall Apart* begins to correct the historical record by retelling the conquest of Africa from Okonkwo's African perspective rather than the District Commissioner's European one.

Mr. Brown

The first white missionary to come to Umuofia, Mr. Brown gains the clan's respect through his calm nature and patience. He neither attacks the tribe's customs nor badgers them to join him. He restrains his overzealous members from harsh tactics. He simply offers education to the Umuofians and their children. The mission is flourishing when Mr. Brown has to leave for health reasons.

The District Commissioner

The District Commissioner arrives in Umuofia at the same time as the missionaries. He and his court messengers—called "Ashy-Buttocks" for the ash-colored shorts they wear—try clansmen for breaking the white man's law. These white men are greatly hated for their arrogance and disrespect for tribal customs.

Ekwefi

Ekwefi, forty-five years old, is Okonkwo's second wife. Although she fell in love with Okonkwo when he won the famous wrestling match, she did not move in with him until she left her husband three years after the contest. Ekwefi had been lovely in her youth, referred to as "Crystal of Beauty." The years have been hard on her. She has become a courageous and strong-willed woman, overcoming disappointment and bitterness in her life. She has borne ten children, only one of whom has lived. She stands up to Okonkwo and lives for her daughter, Ezinma.

Enoch

Enoch is an overzealous member of Mr. Brown's mission. While Mr. Brown restrains Enoch from taking his faith to extremes, Mr. Smith does not. Mr. Smith not only condones Enoch's excessive actions, he encourages them. Enoch instigates the battle between Umuofia and the church by unmasking an egwugwu, or ancestor spirit, during a public ceremony. This is one of the greatest crimes a man could commit.

Ogbuefi Ezeudu

A noble warrior and the oldest man in all the village, Ogbuefi Ezeudu has achieved a rare three titles. He is the one to tell Okonkwo that the tribe has decided to kill Ikemefuna. Ezeudu warns Okonkwo not to be a part of Ikemefuna's death.

At Ezeudu's death, the clan gathers to bid a final sacred tribute to a man who has nearly attained the highest tribal honor—lord of the land. When Okonkwo accidentally kills Ezeudu's son during the ceremony, the clan is horrified. Okonkwo can think only of Ezeudu's warning.

Ezinma

Ekwefi lives for Ezinma, her only living child, her pride and joy. Okonkwo favors his daughter, who is not only as beautiful as her mother once was, but who grows to understand her father and his moods as no one else does. Father and daughter form a special bond. Okonkwo and Ekwefi treat Ezinma like she is their equal rather than their child. They permit her privileges that other family and tribal children are not granted. Okonkwo's only regret towards Ezinma is that she is not a boy.

Ikemefuna

Ikemefuna comes to live with Okonkwo's family as a peace offering from Ikemefuna's home tribe to the Ibo for the killing of a Umuofian daughter. From the beginning, Ikemefuna fills the void in Okonkwo's life that Okonkwo's own son cannot.

Ikemefuna adjusts quickly to his new family and tribe and energetically participates in activities. He earns everyone's love and respect because he is so lively and talented. Only two years older than Nwoye, Ikemefuna already knows much about the world and can do almost anything. He can identify birds, trap rodents, and make flutes. He knows which trees make the best bows and tells delightful folk stories. Okonkwo appreciates Ikemefuna for the example he sets for Nwoye.

Ikemefuna lives with Okonkwo for three years. The tribe then agrees to kill Ikemefuna because the Oracle of the Hills and the Caves has requested it. Ikemefuna's death brings far-reaching consequences.

Nwoye

Okonkwo's son, Nwoye, disappoints him. Nwoye shows all the signs of his grandfather's sensitivity and laziness, and Okonkwo fears that Nwoye will shame the reputable name Okonkwo has worked so hard to achieve. Nwoye knows that he should enjoy the masculine rites of his fellow tribesmen, but he prefers his mother's company and the stories she tells. He questions and is disturbed by many of the tribe's customs. Okonkwo beats and nags Nwoye, making Nwoye more unhappy and further distancing him from the ways of the clan.

When Ikemefuna comes to live with Okonkwo's family, Nwoye grows to admire his knowledge and to love him like a real brother. Out of his respect for Ikemefuna, Nwoye begins to associate more with the men of the family and tribe, and to act more like the man that his father wants him to become.

After Ikemefuna's death, Nwoye feels an emptiness that cannot be filled by the clan's traditions. He is plagued by old questions for which the clan has no answers.

Nwoye's mother

Okonkwo's first wife, Nwoye's mother is wise to the ways of the tribe. While she knows that her sons will never be able to display such emotions, she tells her children wonderful stories that describe feelings like pity and forgiveness. She attempts to keep peace in the family by lying to Okonkwo at times to help the other wives avoid punishment. She tries to adhere to sacred tribal customs. She shows compassion at the message that Ikemefuna is to return to his family. In her own way, Nwoye's mother displays the courage of a tribesman.

Obierika

Obierika is Okonkwo's best friend. Unlike Okonkwo, he is a thinking man. He questions the circumstances that are sending his friend into exile, even while trying to console Okonkwo and taking care of Okonkwo's preparation for departure. Obierika is the one who visits Okonkwo while Okonkwo is exiled. He brings him the first news of the missionaries' arrival, knowing that Okonkwo's son has joined them. At the end of the seven-year exile, Obierika builds Okonkwo two huts and sends for him. Finally, a sad and weary Obierika bids a last tribute to his friend when he leads the diminishing clansmen through the rituals required to cleanse the land Okonkwo has desecrated.

Ojiugo

Ojiugo is Okonkwo's third and youngest wife. She evokes Okonkwo's anger through thoughtless acts and prompts him to break the sacred Week of Peace. As a result, the priest of the earth goddess punishes Okonkwo.

Okonkwo

Out of awe and respect, the Ibo tribe refers to Okonkwo as "Roaring Flame." Fiery of temper with a blazing appearance, Okonkwo strikes fear in the hearts of his clan members as well as his own family unit. Okonkwo's huge build, topped by bushy eyebrows and a very broad nose, give him the look of a tornado on the warpath. His whole demeanor reeks of controlled fury; he even breathes heavily, like a dragon ready to explode. He always appears to be wound for fierce action.

While Okonkwo's appearance portrays a man people fear, it belies the terror Okonkwo hides within himself. For his entire life, Okonkwo has had to deal with having a father who is considered weak and lazy—"agabala" in the tribe's terms. The tribe detests weak, effeminate men. Okonkwo is terrified to think that the tribe will liken him to his father. He is even more afraid of recognizing in himself some semblance of weakness that he sees in his father. Thus, he despises gentleness, idleness, and demonstrations of sensitivity. He will not allow himself to show love, to enjoy the fruits of hard work, or to demonstrate concern for others, nor can he tolerate these in other men. He rules his family unit with an iron fist and expects everyone to act on his commands. He speaks curtly to those he considers less successful than himself and dismisses them as unimportant. An extremely proud man, Okonkwo continually pushes to overcome the image his heredity might have given him.

The tribe sees Okonkwo as powerful. They respect him for his many achievements. Not only has he overcome his father's weaknesses, but also he has accomplished more than the average tribesman. As a young man, he wrestles and beats one of the fiercest fighters in the land. Next, Okonkwo goes on to amass three wives and two barns full of yams. Then, he acquires two titles and is considered the greatest warrior alive.

Mr. Smith

See Reverend James Smith

Reverend James Smith

Mr. Smith replaces Mr. Brown when Mr. Brown has to leave the mission. The Reverend Smith leads the overzealous with a passion. Where Mr. Brown was mild-mannered and quiet, Mr. Smith is angry and flamboyant. He denounces the tribe's customs and bans from his church clan members who must be, according to him, filled with the devil's spirit to want to continue tribal tradition.

Ogbuefi Ugonna

A worthy tribesman of two titles, Ogbuefi Ugonna is one of the first of the village men to receive the sacrament of Holy Communion offered by the Christian missionaries.

Unoka

Unoka is Okonkwo's father, the root of Okonkwo's fear and problems. Unoka represents all that the Ibo abhor—gentleness, lack of ambition, and sensitivity to people and nature. He is a gifted musician who loves fellowship, the change of the seasons, and children. Although Unoka is tall, his stooped posture bears the weight of the tribe's scorn.

Unoka is happy only when he is playing his flute and drinking palm wine. Tribal customs frighten, sicken, and bore him. He hates war and is nauseated by the sight of blood. He would rather make music than grow crops. As a result, his family is more often hungry than not, and he borrows constantly from fellow tribesmen to maintain his household. He dies in disgrace, owing everyone and holding no titles.

Custom and Tradition

Okonkwo's struggle to live up to what he perceives as "traditional" standards of masculinity, and his failure adapt to a changing world, help point out the importance of custom and tradition in the novel. The Ibo tribe defines itself through the ageold traditions it practices in *Things Fall Apart.* While some habits mold tribe members' daily lives, other customs are reserved for special ceremonies. For example, the head of a household honors any male guest by praying over and sharing a kola nut with him, offering the guest the privilege of breaking the nut. They drink palm-wine together, with the oldest person taking the first drink after the provider has tasted it.

Ceremonial customs are more elaborate. The Feast of the New Yam provides an illustration. This Feast gives the tribe an opportunity to thank Ani, the earth goddess and source of all fertility. Preparations for the Feast include thorough hut-cleaning and decorating, cooking, body painting, and head shaving. Relatives come from great distances to partake in the feast and to drink palm-wine. Then, on the second day of the celebration, the great wrestling match is held. The entire village meets in the village playground, or ilo, for the drumming, dancing, and wrestling. The festival continues through the night until the final round is won. Because the tribe views winning a match as a great achievement, the winner earns the tribe's ongoing respect.

Tribal custom dictates every aspect of members' lives. The tribe determines a man's worth by the number of titles he holds, the number of wives he acquires, and the number of yams he grows. The tribe acknowledges a man's very being by the gods' approval of him. Without custom and tradition, the tribe does not exist.

Choices and Consequences

In *Things Fall Apart,* Okonkwo makes a choice early in life to overcome his father's legacy. As a result, Okonkwo gains the tribe's respect through his constant hard work. The tribe rewards him by recognizing his achievements and honoring him as a great warrior. The tribe believes that Okonkwo's personal god, or chi, is good (fate has blessed him). Nevertheless, they realize that Okonkwo has worked hard to achieve all that he has (if a man says yes, his chi says yes). When he breaks the Week of Peace, however, the tribe believes that Okonkwo has begun to feel too self-important and has challenged his chi. They fear the consequences his actions may bring.

The tribe decides to kill Ikemefuna. Even though Ezeudu warns Okonkwo not to be a part of the plan, Okonkwo himself kills Ikemefuna. Okonkwo chooses to kill the boy rather than to appear weak.

When Okonkwo is in exile, he ponders the tribe's view of his chi. He thinks that maybe they have been wrong—that his chi was not made for great things. Okonkwo blames his exile on his chi. He refuses to accept that his actions have led him to this point. He sees no connections among his breaking the Week of Peace, his killing Ikemefuna, and his shooting Ezeudu's son. In Okonkwo's eyes, his troubles result from ill fate and chance.

Topics for Further Study

- How does the displacement from one's culture affect a person psychologically? Explain possible reactions a person might have and the steps someone might take to help him or her adjust.

- School integration is being

attempted across America. How successful has it been? Cite specific examples, such as court cases, to support your answer.

- Integration is being attempted in a high school in Capetown, South Africa. At the beginning of each school day, white students and students from one of the black societies are required to attend a formal assembly. Students are also required to wear school uniforms. What might the students infer from these requirements? Support your answer by discussing the purpose of assemblies and uniforms in our society and researching cultural aspects of one of the black societies in Capetown.

- Compare and contrast American and African colonization by discussing the events and their effects.

- Investigate women's roles in tribal society. Find and discuss specific examples from *Things Fall Apart.*

- Women in tribal societies were often forced to undergo female circumcision. Investigate the purpose of this ritual. What are the medical implications of this procedure?

- Language is an important means of communication as well as a prominent culture marker. What does a person's language tell us about him or her? What effects could loss of one's language—through physical disability or societal disallowance—have on a person?

- Missionaries went to Umuofia to convert the Ibo to Christianity. Should anyone try to change another's religious beliefs? Take a stand from either a Christian's point of view or from an opposite point of view. Prepare a logical argument for presentation in a debate.

- What is the purpose of multicultural education in our country? Describe some of the efforts that are being undertaken by schools around the country. What have been your own experiences? Discuss the methods being used to implement these programs and their success.

Alienation and Loneliness

Okonkwo's exile isolates him from all he has ever known in *Things Fall Apart*. The good name he had built for himself with his tribesmen is a thing of the past. He must start anew. The thought overwhelms him, and Okonkwo feels nothing but despair. Visits from his good friend, Obierika, do little to cheer Okonkwo. News of the white man's intrusion and the tribe's reactions to it disturb him. His distance from the village, and his lack of connection to it, give him a sense of helplessness. Even worse, Okonkwo's son, Nwoye, joins the white man's mission efforts.

Okonkwo's return to the village does nothing to lessen his feelings of alienation and loneliness. The tribe he rejoins is not the same tribe he left. While he does not expect to be received as the respected warrior he once was, he does think that his arrival will prompt an occasion to be remembered. When the clan takes no special notice of his return, Okonkwo realizes that the white man has been too successful in his efforts to change the tribe's ways. Okonkwo grieves the loss of his tribe and the life he once knew. He is not able to overcome his sense of complete alienation.

Betrayal

In *Things Fall Apart,* Okonkwo feels betrayed by his personal god, or chi, which has allowed him to produce a son who is effeminate. Nwoye continually disappoints Okonkwo. As a child, Nwoye prefers his mother's stories to masculine pursuits. As an adult, Nwoye joins the white missionaries.

Okonkwo also feels betrayed by his clan. He

does not understand why his fellow tribesmen have not stood up against the white intruders. When Okonkwo returns from exile, his clan has all but disintegrated. Many of the tribe's leaders have joined the missionaries' efforts; tribal beliefs and customs are being ignored. Okonkwo mourns the death of the strong tribe he once knew and despises the "woman-like" tribe that has taken its place.

Change and Transformation

The tribe to which Okonkwo returns has undergone a complete transformation during his absence in *Things Fall Apart*. The warlike Ibo once looked to its elders for guidance, made sacrifices to gods for deliverance, and solved conflicts though confrontation. Now the Ibo are "woman-like"; they discuss matters among themselves and pray to a god they can not see. Rather than immediately declare war on the Christians when Enoch unmasks the egwugwu, or ancestral spirit, the Ibo only destroy Enoch's compound. Okonkwo realizes how completely the Christians have changed his tribe when the tribesmen allow the remaining court messengers to escape after Okonkwo beheads one of them.

Good and Evil

Many of the tribesmen view the white man as evil in *Things Fall Apart*. Tribesmen did not turn their backs on one another before the white man came. Tribesmen would never have thought to kill their own brothers before the white man came. The arrival of the white man has forced the clan to act in ways that its ancestors deplore. Such evil has never before invaded the clan.

Culture Clash

The arrival of the white man and his culture heralds the death of the Ibo culture in *Things Fall Apart*. The white man does not honor the tribe's customs and strives to convince tribesmen that the white man's ways are better. Achieving some success, the white man encourages the tribesmen who join him, increasing the white man's ranks. As a result, the tribe is split, pitting brother against brother and father against son. Tribal practices diminish as the bond that ties tribesmen deteriorates. Death eventually comes to the weaker of the clashing cultures.

Tragedy

Things Fall Apart chronicles the double tragedies of the deaths of Okonkwo, a revered warrior, and the Ibo, the tribe to which Okonkwo belongs. In literature, tragedy often describes the downfall of a great individual which is caused by a flaw in the person's character. Okonkwo's personal flaw is his unreasonable anger, and his tragedy occurs when the tribe bans him for accidentally killing a young tribesman, and he returns to find a tribe that has changed beyond recognition. The Ibo's public demise results from the destruction of one culture by another, but their tragedy is caused by their turning away from their tribal gods.

Setting

Things Fall Apart is set in Umuofia, a tribal village in the country of Nigeria, in Africa. It is the late 1800s, when English bureaucrats and missionaries are first arriving in the area. There is a long history of conflict between European colonists and the Africans they try to convert and subjegate. But by placing the novel at the beginning of this period Achebe can accentuate the clash of cultures that are just coming into contact. It also sets up a greater contrast between the time Okonkwo leaves the tribe and the time he returns, when his village is almost unrecognizable to him because of the changes brought by the English.

Conflict

In *Things Fall Apart,* the Ibo thrive in Umuofia, practicing ancient rituals and customs. When the white man arrives, however, he ignores the Ibo's values and tries to enforce his own beliefs, laws, and religious practices. Some of the weaker tribesmen join the white man's ranks, leaving gaps in the clan's united front. First, the deserters are impressed with the wealth the white man brings into Umuofia. Second, they find in the white man's religion an acceptance and brotherhood that has never been afforded them due to their lower status in the tribe. As men leave the tribe to become members of the white man's mission, the rift in the tribe widens. Social and psychological conflict abounds as brothers turn their backs on one another, and fathers and sons become strangers.

Narration

Achebe develops *Things Fall Apart* through a third-person narrative—using "he" and "she" for exposition—rather than having the characters tell it themselves. Often speaking in the past tense, he also narrates the story with little use of character dialogue. The resulting story reads like an oral tale that has been passed down through generations of storytellers.

Imagery

While the characters in *Things Fall Apart* have little dialogue, the reader still has a clear image of them and is able to understand their motives. Achebe accomplishes this through his combination of the English language with Ibo vocabulary and proverbs. When the characters do talk, they share the rich proverbs that are "the palm-oil with which words are eaten." Achebe uses the proverbs not only to illustrate his characters but also to paint pictures of the society he is depicting, to reveal themes, and to develop conflict. Vivid images result, giving the reader a clear representation of people and events.

Point of View

Critics praise Achebe for his adept shifts in point of view in *Things Fall Apart.* Achebe begins the story from Okonkwo's point of view. Okonkwo's story helps the reader understand the Ibo's daily customs and rituals as well as celebrations for the main events in life: birth, marriage, and death. As the story progresses, however, it becomes more the clan's story than Okonkwo's personal story. The reader follows the clan's life, gradual disintegration, and death. The novel becomes one of situation rather than character; the reader begins to feel a certain sympathy for the tribe instead of the individual. The final shift occurs when Achebe ends the story from the District Commissioner's viewpoint. While some critics feel that Achebe's ending lectures, others believe that it strengthens the conclusion for the reader. Some even view it as a form of functionalism, an African tradition of cultural instruction.

Plot and Structure

Divided into three parts, *Things Fall Apart* comprises many substories. Yet Achebe holds the various stories together through his use of proverbs, traditional oral tales, and *leitmotif,* or recurring images or phrases. Ibo proverbs occur throughout the book, providing a unity to the surface progression of the story. For example, "when a man says yes, his chi says yes" is the proverb the tribe applies to Okonkwo's success, on the one hand, but is also the proverb Okonkwo, himself, applies to his failure. Traditional oral tales always contain a tale within the tale. Nwoye's mother is an expert at telling these tales—morals embedded in stories. The stories Achebe tells throughout *Things Fall Apart* are themselves tales within the tale. Leitmotif is the association of a repeated theme with a particular idea. Achebe connects masculinity with land, yams, titles, and wives. He repeatedly associates this view of masculinity with a certain stagnancy in Umuofia. While a traditional Western plot may not be evident in *Things Fall Apart,* a definite structure with an African flavor lends itself to the overall unity of the story.

Foil

Achebe uses foil—a type of contrast—to strengthen his primary characters in *Things Fall Apart,* illuminating their differences. The following pairs of characters serve as foils for each other: Okonkwo and Obierika, Ikemefuna and Nwoye, and Mr. Brown and the Reverend Smith. Okonkwo rarely thinks; he is a man of action. He follows the tribe's customs almost blindly and values its opinion of him over his own good sense. Obierika, on the other hand, ponders the things that happen to Okonkwo and his tribe. Obierika often makes his own decisions and wonders about the tribe's wisdom in some of its actions. Ikemefuna exemplifies the rising young tribesman. A masculine youth, full of energy and personality, Ikemefuna participates in the manly activities expected of him. In contrast, Nwoye appears lazy and effeminate. He prefers listening to his mother's stories over making plans for war. He detests the sight of blood and abhors violence of any kind. Mr. Brown speaks gently and restrains the overzealous members of his mission from overwhelming the clan. He seeks to win the people over by offering education and sincere faith. The Reverend Smith is the fire-and-brimstone preacher who replaces Mr. Brown. He sees the world in black and white; either something is evil, or it is good. He thrives on his converts' zeal and encourages them to do whatever it takes to gain supporters for his cause.

Tribal Society

Things Fall Apart was published in 1958 just prior to Nigerian independence, but it depicts precolonial Africa. Achebe felt it was important to portray Nigerians as they really were—not just provide a shallow description of them as other authors had. The story takes place in the typical tribal village of Umuofia, where the inhabitants (whom Achebe calls the Ibo, but who are also known as the Igbo) practice rituals common to their native traditions.

The Ibo worshipped gods who protect, advise, and chastise them and who are represented by priests and priestesses within the clan. For example, the Oracle of the Hills and the Caves grants knowledge and wisdom to those who are brave enough to consult him. No one has ever seen the Oracle except his priestess, who is an Ibo woman who has special powers of her own. Not only did the gods advise the Ibo on community matters, but also they guided individuals. Each person had a personal god, or chi, that directed his or her actions. A strong chi meant a strong person; people with weak chis were pitied. Each man kept a separate hut, or shrine, where he stored the symbols of his personal god and his ancestral spirits.

A hunting and gathering society, the Ibo

existed on vegetables, with yams as the primary crop. Yams were so important to them that the Ibo celebrated each new year with the Feast of the New Yam. This festival thanked Ani, the earth goddess and source of all fertility. The Ibo prepared for days for the festival, and the celebration itself lasted for two days. Yams also played a part in determining a man's status in the tribe—the more yams a man has, the higher his status. Trade with other villages was facilitated by small seashells called cowries which were used as a form of currency.

Within the village, people were grouped according to families, with the eldest man in the family having the most power. On matters affecting the whole village, an assembly of adult men debated courses of action, and men could influence these assemblies by purchasing "titles" from the tribal elders. This system encouraged hard work and the spread of wealth. People who transgressed against the laws and customs of the village had to confront the egwugwu, an assembly of tribesmen masked as spirits, who would settle disputes and hand out punishment. Individual villages also attained various degrees of political status. In the novel, other tribes respect and fear Umuofia. They believe that Umuofia's magic is powerful and that the village's war-medicine, or agadinwayi, is particularly potent. Neighboring clans always try to settle disputes peacefully with Umuofia to avoid having to war with them.

Christianity and Colonization

While Christianity spread across North and South Africa as early as the late fifteenth century, Christianity took its strongest hold when the majority of the missionaries arrived in the late 1800s. After centuries of taking slaves out of Africa, Britain had outlawed the slave trade and now saw the continent as ripe for colonization. Missionaries sent to convert the local population were often the first settlers. They believed they could atone for the hoffors of slavery by saving the souls of Africans.

At first, Africans were mistrustful of European Christians, and took advantage of the education the missionaries provided without converting. Individuals who had no power under the current tribal order, however, soon converted; in the novel, the missionaries who come to Umuofia convert only the weaker tribesmen, or efulefu. Missionaries would convince these tribesmen that their tribe worshipped false gods and that its false gods did not have the ability to punish them if they chose to join the mission. When the mission and its converts accepted even the outcasts of the clan, the missionaries' ranks grew. Eventually, some of the more important tribesmen would convert. As the mission expanded, the clan divided, discontent simmered, and conflicts arose.

English Bureaucrats and Colonization

After the arrival of the British, when conflicts

came up between villages the white government would intervene instead of allowing villagers to settle them themselves. In the novel, a white District Commissioner brings with him court messengers whose duty it is to bring in people who break the white man's law. The messengers, called "Ashy-Buttocks" for the ash-colored shorts they wear, are hated for their high-handed attitudes. These messengers and interpreters were often African Christian converts who looked down on tribesmen who still followed traditional customs. If violence involved any white missionaries or bureaucrats, British soldiers would often slaughter whole villages instead of seeking and punishing guilty individuals. The British passed an ordinance in 1912 that legalized this practice, and during an uprising in 1915, British troops killed more than forty natives in retaliation for one dead and one wounded British soldier.

One of the most important results of Europe's colonization of Africa was the division of Africa into at least fifty nation-states. Rather than being a part of a society determined by common language and livelihood, Africans lived according to political boundaries. The divisions often split ethnic groups, leading to tension and sometimes violence. The cohesiveness of the traditional society was gone.

Compare & Contrast

- **1800s:** Prior to colonization, common language and geography differentiated African societies. Six types of societies existed: hunting and gathering societies, cattle-herding societies, forest dwellers, fishermen, grain-raising societies, and city (urban) societies. The geographic area in which people lived determined their lifestyle.

Colonial Africa: Africa was divided into more than fifty nation-states, with no regard for maintaining groups sharing common language and livelihood.

Today: Societies are no longer as clear-cut. People have more opportunities for education, better jobs, and improved means of communication and transportation. They marry individuals from other societies. As a result, the societies have become mixed, but ethnic conflicts still lead to violence.

- **1800s:** While religion varied from society to society, most Africans shared some common beliefs and practices. They believed in a supreme creator god or spirit. Other lesser gods revealed themselves as, and worked through, community ancestors.

  Colonial Africa: Missionaries arrived and introduced Christianity. Many tribesmen converted to the new religion.

Today: While more than an estimated 25% of Africa is Christian, traditional African religion is still practiced, as is Islam. Islam is a monotheistic religion related to the Jewish and Christian traditions.

- **1800s:** Prior to colonization, Africans had their own identities and cultures and were not concerned with participating in the modern world.

  Colonial Africa: After colonization, African children were taught European history and literature so that they might compete in the modern world, while their own heritage was ignored.

  Today: Africans continue to seek the independence they began to achieve in the 1950s and 1960s. There is, however, a renewed interest in cultural heritage, and traditional customs are being taught to African children.

Nigerian Independence

British colonial rule in Nigeria lasted only fifty-seven years, from 1903 to 1960. Although

Nigerians had long called for self-rule, it was not until the end of World War II that England began heeding these calls. The Richards Constitution of 1946 was the first attempt to grant some native rule by bringing the diverse peoples of Nigeria under one representative government. The three regions (northern, southern and western) were brought under the administration of one legislative council composed of twenty-eight Nigerians and seventeen British officers. Regional councils, however, guaranteed some independence from the national council and forged a link between local authorities, such as tribal chiefs, and the national government. There were three major tribes (the Hausa, the Yoruba and the Igbo) and more than eight smaller ones living in Nigeria. This diversity complicated the creation of a unified Nigeria. Between 1946 and 1960 the country went through several different constitutions, each one attempting to balance power between the regional and the national bodies of government.

On October 1, 1960, Nigeria attained full status as a sovereign state and a member of the British Commonwealth. But under the Constitution of 1960 the Queen of England was still the head of state. She remained the commander-in-chief of Nigeria's armed forces, and the Nigerian navy operated as part of Britain's Royal Navy. Nigerians felt frustrated by the implication that they were the subjects of a monarch living over 4,000 miles away. In 1963, five years after the publication of Achebe's novel, a new constitution would replace the British monarch with a Nigerian president as head of state in Nigeria.

Literary Traditions

Achebe wrote *Things Fall Apart* just before Nigeria received its independence. He intended the book for audiences outside Africa; he wanted to paint a true picture of precolonial Africa for those people who had no direct knowledge of traditional African societies. As a result of the Nigerians' acquisition of independence, the Nigerian educational system sought to encourage a national pride through the study of Nigerian heritage. The educational system required Achebe's book in high schools throughout the English-speaking countries in Africa. The book was well received. Chinua Achebe has been recognized as "the most original African novelist writing in English," according to Charles Larson in *The Emergence of African Fiction.* Critics throughout the world have praised *Things Fall Apart* as the first African English-language classic.

Critical Overview

Things Fall Apart has experienced a huge success. Since it was published in 1958, the book has sold more than two million copies in over thirty languages. Critics attribute its success not only to the book's message, but also to Achebe's talents as a writer. Achebe believes that stories should serve a purpose; they should deliver a meaningful message to the people who hear or read them. When Achebe wrote *Things Fall Apart,* his intent was to explain the beginnings of the turmoil Africans have been experiencing over the past century. He wanted to describe the integrity of precolonial Nigeria, detail the effects of colonialism on tribal societies, and reveal the kinds of immoral treatment that people in modern society are often made to suffer. Critics agree that he accomplished all of these purposes. They feel that he writes honestly about tribal life and the colonial legacy. They also believe that Achebe delivers another important message: man will always face change, and he who can accommodate change will survive.

While some readers will view Okonkwo's deterioration and demise as a tragic result of his going against the will of the gods, others see the new "world order" as inevitable. Okonkwo's acts do not bring the tribe to an end; it is the tribe's lack of adaptability that destroys it. These opposing interpretations strengthen the impact of the book. In *The Growth of the African Novel,* Eustace Palmer states that "while deploring the imperialists' brutality and condescension, [Achebe] seems to suggest that change is inevitable and wise men ... reconcile themselves to accommodating change. It is the diehards ... who resist and are destroyed in the process."

Achebe successfully communicates his message through skillful writing. From the time critics first read his book, they have concurred that Achebe's craftsmanship earns him a place among the best writers in the world. An example of his craftsmanship is Achebe's ability to convey the essence of traditional Nigeria while borrowing from the conventions of the European novel. He was the first Nigerian writer to adapt African oral tradition to novel form. In doing so, "he created a new novel that possesses its own autonomy and transcends the limits set by both his African and European teachers," as Kofi Awoonor observes in *The Breast of the Earth.* The borrowed European elements Achebe contrasts are communal life over the individual character and the beauty and detail of traditional tribal life over brief references to background. His descriptions of day-to-day life and special ceremonial customs provide a "powerful presentation of the beauty, strength, and validity of traditional life and values," as Palmer observes.

Literary experts also point out Achebe's ability to combine language forms, maintain thematic unity, and shape conflict in *Things Fall Apart.* His use of Ibo proverbs in conjunction with the English language places the reader in Africa with the Ibo tribe. Adrian A. Roscoe explains in his book *Mother Is Gold: A Study of West African Literature,* "Proverbs are cherished by Achebe's people as tribal heirlooms, the treasure boxes of their cultural heritage." In addition, the combination of languages helps reiterate the theme of tradition versus change. Roscoe goes on to say, "Through [proverbs] traditions are received and handed on; and when they disappear or fall into disuse ... it is a sign that a particular tradition, or indeed a whole way of life, is passing away."

The death of the language then, a powerful cultural tradition, signifies the ultimate discord in the novel—the fall of one culture to another. G. D. Killam observes in *The Novels of Chinua Achebe* that "the conflict in the novel, vested in Okonkwo, derives from the series of crushing blows which are levelled at traditional values by an alien and more powerful culture causing, in the end, the traditional society to fall apart." Achebe's mastery of content and his talent as a writer contribute to his world-wide success with this novel as well as his other novels, articles, poems, and essays. As Killam concludes, his writing conveys that "the spirit of man and the belief in the possibility of triumph endures."

Sources

Kofi Awoonor, *The Breast of the Earth,* Doubleday, 1975.

G. D. Killam, *The Novels of Chinua Achebe,* Africana Publishing, 1969.

Charles Larson, "Chinua Achebe's 'Things Fall Apart': The Archetypal African Novel" and "Characters and Modes of Characterization: Chinua Achebe, James Ngugi, and Peter Abrahams," in *The Emergence of African Fiction,* revised edition, Indiana University Press, 1972, pp. 27–65, 147–66.

Eustace Palmer, *The Growth of the African Novel,* Heinemann, 1979.

Adrian A. Roscoe, *Mother Is Gold: A Study of West African Literature,* Cambridge University Press, 1971.

For Further Study

Chinua Achebe, "The Novelist as Teacher," in *Hope and Impediments: Selected Essays,* Anchor Books, 1988, pp. 40–46.

> Achebe's own explanation of the social significance of his fiction.

Edna Aizenberg, "The Third World Novel as Counterhistory: *Things Fall Apart* and Asturias's *Men of Maize,"* in *Approaches to Teaching Achebe's "Things Fall Apart,"* edited by Bemth Lindfors, Modern Language Association of America, 1991, pp. 85–90.

> An analysis of how *Things Fall Apart* revises biased colonial histories.

Ernest N. Emenyonu, "Chinua Achebe's *Things Fall Apart:* A Classic Study in Colonial Diplomatic Tactlessness," in *Chinua Achebe: A Celebration,* edited by Kirsten Holst Petersen and Anna Rutherford, Heinemann, 1990, pp. 83–88.

> An analysis of the political significance of *Things Fall Apart* as a critique of colonialism.

Abiola Irele, "The Tragic Conflict in the Novels of Chinua Achebe," in *Critical Perspectives on Chinua Achebe,* edited by C. L. Innes and Bernth Lindfors, Three Continents Press, 1978, pp. 10–21.

An analysis of Achebe's use of tragedy.

Solomon O. lyasere, "Narrative Techniques in *Things Fall Apart,*" in *Critical Perspectives on Chinua Achebe,* edited by C. L. Innes and Bernth Lindfors, Three Continents Press, 1978, pp. 92–110.

> A general introduction to the themes and narrative structure of *Things Fall Apart.*

Abdul JanMohamed, "Sophisticated Primitivism: The Syncretism of Oral and Literate Modes in Achebe's *Things Fall Apart,*" *Ariel: A Review of International English Literature,* Vol. 15, No. 4, 1984, pp. 19–39.

> An analysis of how Achebe synthesizes African oral cultural traditions with English literary conventions.

Biodun Jeyifo, "Okonkwo and His Mother: *Things Fall Apart* and Issues of Gender in the Constitution of African Postcolonial Discourse," in *Callaloo: A Journal of African-American and Afrrican Arts and Letters,* Vol. 16,No.4,1993, pp. 847–58.

> An analysis of the role of gender in *Things Fall Apart.*

Bernth Lindfors, "The Palm-Oil with Which Achebe's Words are Eaten," in *African Literature Today,* Vol. 1,1968, pp. 3–18.

> An analysis of Achebe's use of traditional proverbs in *Things Fall*

Apart.

Alastair Niven, "Chinua Achebe and the Possibility of Modern Tragedy," in *Chinua Achebe: A Celebration,* edited by Kirsten Holst Petersen and Anna Rutherford, Heinemann, 1990, pp. 41–50.

> An analysis of Achebe's use of tragedy.

Emmanuel Obiechina, "Narrative Proverbs in the African Novel," *Research in African Literatures,* Vol. 24, No. 4, 1993, pp. 123–40.

> An analysis of Achebe's use of African oral cultural traditions such as proverbs and storytelling.

Ato Quayson, "Realism, Criticism, and the Disguises of Both: A Reading of Chinua Achebe's *Things Fall Apart* with an Evaluation of the Criticism Relating to It," in *Research in African Literatures,* Vol. 25, No. 4, 1994, pp. 117–36.

> Argues that most critics have emphasized the realistic dimensions of *Things Fall Apart* without adequately discussing how the novel has its own biased perspective.

Joseph Swann, "From *Things Fall Apart* to *Anthills of the Savannah:* The Changing Face of History in Chinua Achebe's Novels," in *Crisis and Creativity in the New Literatures in English,* edited by Geoffrey V. Davis and Hena Maes-Jelinek, Rodopi, 1990, pp. 191–203.

> An analysis of how Achebe's

approach to history changes in each of his novels.

CPSIA information can be obtained
at www.ICGtesting.com
Printed in the USA
LVOW13s1746311017
554455LV00010B/608/P